I Am Me

Affirmations for Children

Erin Toner
Illustrated by Eminence System

Illustrations by Eminence System
Book design by Sarah E. Holroyd (https://sleepingcatbooks.com)

ISBN: 978-1-7775511-0-0 (paperback)
ISBN: 978-1-7775511-1-7 (hardcover)

Juvenile nonfiction

Wonder Child Publications
British Columbia, Canada

For my daughter, who opened my eyes
to a whole new world of imagination.

For my parents, who always believed
in me, gave me wings to fly, and told
me I could be anything I wanted to be.

I am Capable

Just like all boys and girls

I am Honest

I always try to do what is right

I am **Loving**

I live each day with love,
from morning to night

I make mistakes

and I know that is Okay

I am always **Learning**

I try my hardest every day

I **Believe** in myself

I show the world I am tough

I Stand Up for myself

I protect myself and I speak my Truth

I stand up for people
Everywhere

because it's the
right thing to do

I take good Care of my body and mind

because there is

only one of Me

I have a lot of **Joy** in my heart

A **Light** to shine for the world to see

It's as big as an ocean

It stretches from the earth to the clouds above

My mind is Strong

It's wide open to
learn new ideas

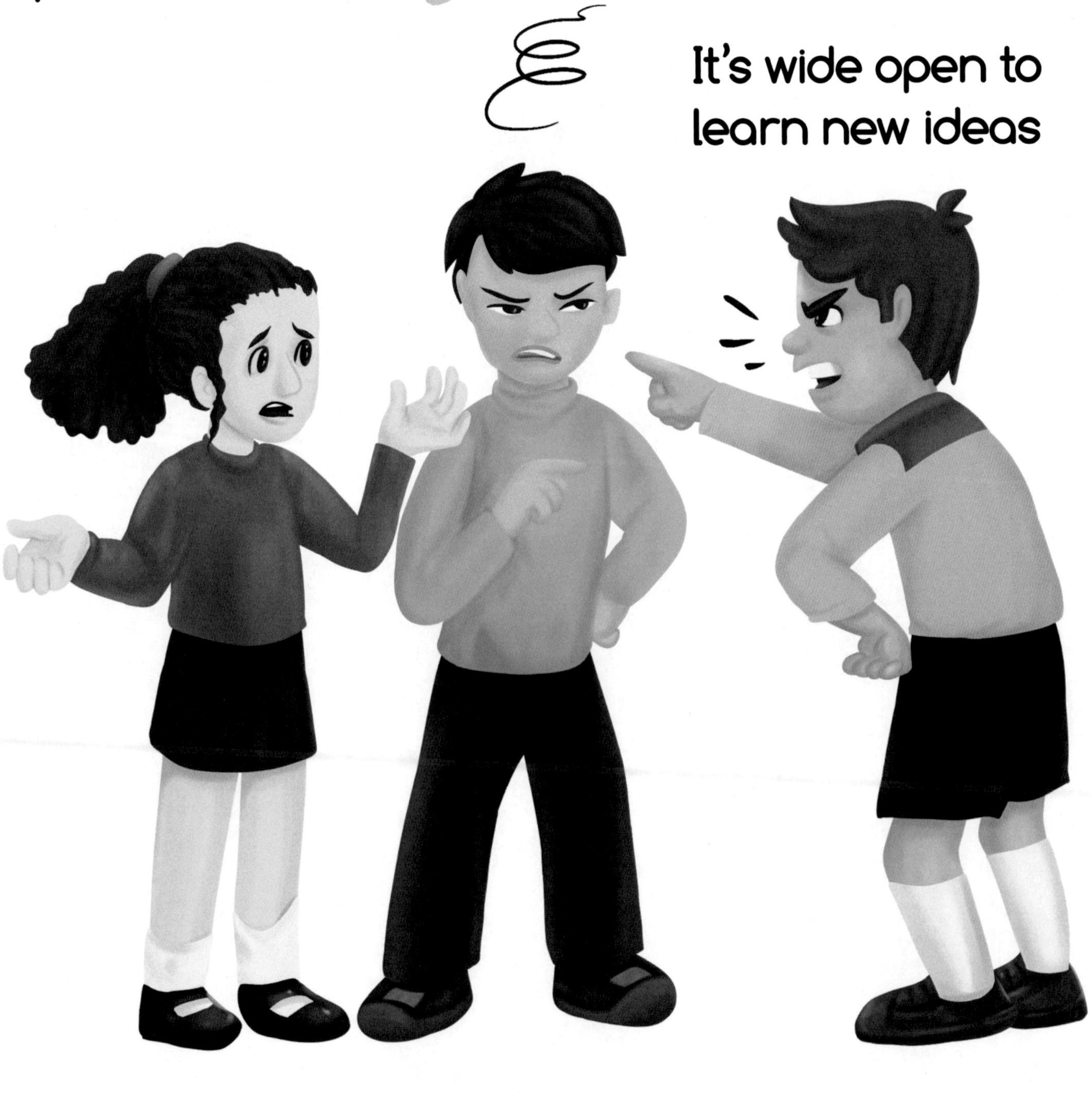

It's strong enough to understand

HA HA HA HA

That there will always be differences between us

Each day I am kind to everyone I meet

For I am **Love** and you are too

I can **Change** the world
By taking steps big and small

More Affirmations!

Here are some more affirmations you can say with your parents! Choose different ones each day that will help with how you are feeling.

I am strong
I am brave
I am kind
I am loving
I love every part of myself
I take good care of my body and my mind
I am full of light
I shine my light for all the world to see
I set a good example for others
I make mistakes and that is okay
I can do anything I set my mind to do
I believe in myself
I am in charge of my thoughts
I am in charge of how I react in all situations
I can do hard things
I am worthy of greatness
I am enough
I can change the world

You are you!

Now it's your turn! Come up with your own unique and special affirmations and write them on this page.

I _____

I _____

I _____

I _____

I _____

I _____

I _____

I _____

I _____

I _____

I _____

I _____

I _____

I _____

About the Creators

Erin Toner

Erin lives in British Columbia, Canada, where she spends a lot of time in nature. She loves to learn about the environment around her and all of the incredible creatures who live there. Erin loves to write stories for children. She is the author of this book and others from Wonder Child Publications.

Erin thanks you for reading this book and encourages you to share your light and positivity with your friends!

Eminence System

Eminence System is a team of illustrators based in Kolkata, India. They specialize in children's book illustrations, concept characters, colouring books, avatars, mascots, comic books, game assets, and more. They brought Erin's book to life with beautiful illustrations.

Made in the USA
Middletown, DE
22 March 2021

35362277R00018